No Third Thing

poems by

Tess Kincaid

Finishing Line Press
Georgetown, Kentucky

No Third Thing

ACKNOWLEDGMENTS

I would like to extend my appreciation to the readers of *Tess Abroad*
and *Magpie Tales* blogs for their kind and generous support.

Editor: Christen Kincaid

Cover Art: Tess Kincaid

Author Photo: Tess Kincaid

Cover Design: Elizabeth Maines

Printed in the USA on acid-free paper.
Order online: www.finishinglinepress.com
also available on amazon.com

Author inquiries and mail orders:
Finishing Line Press
P. O. Box 1626
Georgetown, Kentucky 40324
U. S. A.

Table of Contents

For Robin, with love

Morning Star

Venus whispers through limbs in the ash;
charts the path of twinkle, twinkle, little.
Yet so much.

What are you like?

Sleep becomes a nuisance.
I pace the ceiling, press warm footprints
to the windowpane, count the night
on her glow-in-the-dark rosary,
string it bead by bead across the sea.

Her morning eye watches from a headless torso,
holds me, transfixed.
My goddess of love and war devotes herself
to the small hours,
offers me your kiss.

She is darling,
but not as dear as you.

Insouciance

I leave the bed unmade—
toss the duvet to the floor,

leave it, rumpled and quiet,
along with my mother's hysteria.

The unholy mess coddles tomorrow
with pillow whispered yes.

I have slept with you for years—
pink menagerie of primitive art,

socks lost, one at a time,
in fanciful fruit-spilled sheets.

There is not my side or yours—
I stretch out in the center.

The Morn's Night

An hour ago,
I was a child of fables,
pokeweed.

A tongue roller,
chewer of grass—
I could graft an oak from a twig.

Meanwhile, it's another o'clock;
acorns drop from grown trees.

The moon bellows baritone;
omits the chorus,
replaces it with zees.

Vitruvian sweetness finds me,
springing spreadeagle—
wheel of honeysuckle.

I forget sleep;
shake out the pillowcase,
wrap it around my head
for a babushka—

sound a klaxon,
hail a hackney carriage.

Get to Falkirk.

Whether

Our ritual forecast:
clouds in northern parts

discussed a dozen charming ways.
I tell you nonchalantly

how windows rattle,
twister of the decade roars in my chair.

You do not realize Fahrenheit;
move knee-deep in symphony,

arrange the tempest of my own making,
envelop me in temperate.

No matter how hard we try
we cannot ignore stray raindrops.

I look at you with frankness;
ask whether or not it is now.

Spherical

There is exotic in repeating,
pouring in a censer.
Swinging lasso, carefree.

It floats circular, heady, hypnotic;
pollinating everything open in my wake.
Ritual of joy.

This time, I am brave enough
to leave nothing unsaid; the whole
makes cosmic sense.

Orbed. Embraceable.

I am compelled to whisper it in round.
A chant. Maybe a prayer,
on the brink of a spell.

Feather

I watch the sky,
listen for you in the wind,
shake out my hair, open my shirt,
let rain have its way.
Shy clouds cover their eyes.

I pick up a pleasurable stone,
one you might choose to skip;
suck April from it,
taste distant fault lines,
hold it in the roof of my mouth.

I find a lone feather,
think how it floated down,
like a sleek ghost
from something wild, airborne.
Looks right in my hair.

I wait for light to change,
this stubborn season to end,
for a massive earthquake
to come to my assistance.

Flight

Pilot me to the edge,
to the door between either and or.

Wear tie and handkerchief,
the trilby that looks sexier on you—
with midnight in your pocket,
your shadow fixed between the arrows.

Look to the middle distance when the tide is out—
at last you see migration on the horizon.

Give me mellow, for keeps.
Show me the other side of clouds—
pull goggles over my eyes,
kisses from my quiver.

Let me be free to let go—
die that little death

Foxed

Someone made a wish,
pressed a flower,
left a tear on the page,
below trees
slashed with names,
hearts cut in bark. Splashed
river water. Catfish.
Cat hair. Dog-eared.

Pocked yellow pencil. Scribbles.
Foxed. Cough in a concert, a kiss.
A single glove.
Cigarette ash dropped
Hansel & Gretel style
up frayed steps
to a lover's room.
Wood sighs. Sheets twist.
Sock with a hole. Rain.

Mud. Drainpipes.
Brave earthy things. You.
Damp. Preferably mellow,
a little bit worn.

Your Face

The first time
nostalgia came over me;
like looking at a picture of myself
I had never seen.

I gazed, second person,
mute, hungry voyeur;
your suited and booted margins
pleasingly familiar.

Something sexy happened.

Your eyes spoke;
I could lip-read them.
Hush! this is the year of the tiger.
Let's lunch forever.

Now, a visual condiment;
ferocious but pensive,
piquant, like ketchup
with an indefinite shelf life.

Kensington

There were paving stones,
a menu in a glass case,
steps descending.

You were with her,
smoking among checkered tables,
trembling candles. Wine.

Our eyes met over shoulders,
forkfuls of spaghetti.
Her back to me, his to you.

It didn't matter what you were saying.
Your occasional smile spoke
between gestures.

I wondered: which flat
you would return to; if you had a cat;
what album you would choose.

Had I known it was you
I would have stopped for a kiss
on the way out.

Wanderlust

I return. Two if by sea.
God-force without a compass.
Not for homesickness.
I have no real place.

The rail acts as stylus.
Dirty crackle. Hiss of anticipation.
I board a north boat with lanterns.
Gulls in my wake.

The edge of the world knows
the songs of my heavy-booted fathers.
Cliffs rise to welcome me.
Oceanic. Colder than pewter.

Wyeth skies find a home
on the other side of the Atlantic.
I see an unknown soldier in the clouds,
covered with a greatcoat.

He whispers. *Mainland.*
Welcomes me with a wheelhouse.
Offers cake. A pillow for my head.
Shows me the next bend in the road.

Lighthouse

Before I open my eyes
I hear the call of waves,
the moan of timber.

I had forgotten there would be gulls,
the innocence of sea air
on my pillow.

It breathes differently, virginal;
never inhaled
by anyone else.

I consider drowning;
I don't cry out
or wave my arms.

There is no anchor;
sighs from my lips and nose
rhythm the stillness.

The keeper stirs;
tends the flame; ensures
a safe and pleasant passage.

60 Degrees North

Oarsmen heave
nets of mackerel
from cast-iron waves;

half-booted and silent,
they have no need to tell stories,
ask *dus du mind?*

how after creation God gathered
leftover shards, pressed them together
to make the hilt of a sword.

Women rule the shore,
croon grounded wool and songs
scented with the whisky of a peat fire,

watch the sliver of land
between water and cloud,
lightning rod of the far edge;

where men pull and point like compasses,
breathe in the charge of sea,
think nothing of rocks.

Atlantic Waves

In the space between the crash
and pull of this wave,
I hand you a landlocked heart,
chest deep, tumbled
incandescent as sea glass.

Turn it over,
examine it
in the palm of your hand.
See how important it is,
how far it traveled.

Press it
to your lips,
feel the soft-spoken stone
whisper bottle green
in your listening mouth.

Let it dissolve whole,
release the saved-up thirst,
the delicate, jellied passion.
All you hear is the sea.
Nothing else matters.

Sexton

The shutters are open,
there are no curtains.

Stop. Look through the dark pane.
Find simple sanctuary without icon or lace,

a congregation of one, who has forgotten
how to pray. Come. Listen.

Take up residence, sweep away the dust;
expose silent eyes, deep wits.

Light a candle. Line the sills with potted geraniums.
Stay. Long enough to see them grow.

Be the sexton who makes supper of thoughts,
whisks a fluffy omelet of the past.

Sing. Something that sounds like a hymn,
what ships and stones might say.

Dote on my still possible body,
the soft secret structure of worship.

Shoot

Dusk is recommended
for modest petticoats.
For best light, wait for the sun
to leave its comfort zone.

Capture rhapsody
in more pixels than God.
Press your head against the earth.
Feel the rhythm.

Coax summer percussion.
Join the conga. Be seen on the street.
Peonies wear long-stemmed heels.
Ants pluck them tom-tom pink.

Look deeper than June,
past chlorophyll and bees.
Stop searching for color.
Think dappled things.

Roses strut runway red.
Shoot them in monochrome.

Vitamin

I was anemic:
smelling of mothballs,
cluttered with rejections,
unpaid bills, tired blood,
years of night.

Now a daily swallow.
Kiss swished down with promise.
You taste better than any placebo.
Rinse life clean.
Float. Gulp.

I am dependent.
Convinced you impact mortality.
Supplement everything.
Give me injections.
A horse pill.

Remittance Man

This morning I dream you wear your hat;
the well-loved trilby that accompanied you
to the King George, where three-year olds meet
older horses.

You stand quietly, hands across your chest.
I imagine you posed like that,
calmly watching the 3:10; cigarette dangling
from your whiskers.

I step from behind, hand on your shoulder,
remove the hat, place it cocked over my eye.
All its privileges and undeniable luck released
upon my head.

Regular Melancholy

There must be something
other than ringtones.
I need freedom with a heavy clapper.
The steeple in my road is silent.
You show me a cathedral with a crown,
tell me about the chimes.
A flat, E flat, A flat, C. Ascending.
I find the notes on the piano,
imagine the clang of hours. A clock,
not yet time. Pick my thumbnail
like a dewclaw. Crave
a farm bell, a cowbell. Anything
but this incessant death knell.

Inked

Bows and arrows rise
in blue-painted memory,
whisper secrets in a language
that no longer exists.

I am compelled to tattoo
Pictish letters on my skin,
preserve the modern heir
of a distant arsenal.

Midnight ink voices
another century,
another continent;
marks my rite of passage.

It tells the story of us:
connections and parallels
in endless equinox—
a barcode to identify me as yours.

Found

There are dozens.
Unearthed. Scrappy.
I open the door.
Some try to get out.

Casanova figure-eights,
makes love to my boots.
Fat one naps in a hammock,
another watches from the eaves.

Then there is you. Waiting.

I practice this moment in my head,
half-remembered. Silent.
Nostalgia draws us, deliberate,
as if we have always.

I hold you, feel the scratch.
Look in your melancholy eyes.
Tell me everything.
I like to be sad.

Zebra

We wear a zebra suit.
Taunt cats at the zoo.

You are the head. Tell the joke
about black and white and red.

(Embarrassed) I shake our tail.
Rattle the cage with our hind legs.

They pace. Look at us.
A sandwich. Chain gang of two.

Bow their heads. (Say grace)
by his stripes we are healed.

Warning sign. Loose letters.
Beyond this: the point of no return.

(Without our glasses) squinting
gets us nowhere. And everywhere.

We wear a zebra suit.
Share some striped pajamas.

Yellow House

I lie with insomnia,
wishing it was you.
Listen as salt trucks echo
along the river road;
dare to disturb monochrome.

The autumn of me craves
orange marmalade on toast,
breakfast with no conversation,
watching sunflowers
grow into firm-fleshed love children.

I think about Vincent nibbling his paint,
how the taste of his favorite
floated vivid on his tongue,
how he was happiest
in the yellow house.

Settlement of Snow

Boots tramp your arrival.
I am aware of you.
Wyeth stillness lies
in the bodice of my gown.
Unlace the corset with gloved hands
to find the curvature of the earth.

Fire hisses.

Impatient embers
find their way into everything we know.
The room is overwarm.
Gathered branches tumble to the floor.
There is no script, no canvas.
This is no ordinary happiness.

Explicit Cake

Progression of days playing
in a constant loop,
a marriage of minds.

The loop is safe;
just what we take,
walking all that is left.

Time hangs in the air.
Oceans dry up.

Paths wind in sentences,
give rabbits chase,
willow to climb.

Curves follow a mutual train,
pause for picnic lunch,
explicit cake.

Done with doing, I wait
for the loop to be installed
permanently; with no way out,

a cul-de-sac.

No Third Thing

Only so much room in a lifeboat,
half-capacity sixareen. Bushel basket.
Butcher. Baker. Maybe
a candlestick-maker;
the notables cross over
in threesomes.

Synchronicities flutter in threes,
casually. Historically informed,
hinting at world harmony;
a table of elements
that dissolves on the tongue
like rice paper, moths.

This time it's fresh;
just the northeast wind.
Ball of string. Buttermilk sky.
A buoyant list scrawled
on a paper kite:

1. I am loved
2. There is solace

There is no third thing.

T ess Kincaid is the author of two other collections of poetry, including *Patina*, chosen as semi-finalist in the Finishing Line Press Open Chapbook competition, and *Unpressed*. Her poems have appeared in *Painted Bride Quarterly*, *Iodine Poetry Journal*, and *Ohio Poetry Association Anthology*.

As founder of *Magpie Tales* interactive creative writing blog, she is passionate about investing in the international writing community. She posts new work and reviews on her blog *Tess Abroad*.